A 31-year-old British-Indian poet based in Berlin, **Nisha Bhakoo** has been published widely in literary magazines and anthologies, and given readings internationally, including at BAFTA and the Ledbury Poetry Festival. She was shortlisted for Cambridge University's Jane Martin Poetry Prize, and awarded third prize in the Ledbury Poetry Competition for her poem 'Five Throats' in 2015. She was also selected for the GlogauAIR artist residency in Berlin. Her poetry films and collages have been exhibited in both the UK and Germany, and she had a solo exhibition at Rich Mix, London, in winter 2015.

YOU FOUND A BEATING HEART

NISHA BHAKOO

Ⓣ The Onslaught Press

Published in Oxford by The Onslaught Press
11 Ridley Road, OX4 2QJ
September, 2016

℗

Texts © 2016 **Nisha Bhakoo**

Cover, illustrations & this edition © 2016 **Mathew Staunton**

ISBN: **978-0-9934217-7-8**

Typeset in Akira Kobayashi's **Din Next** & Christ Burke's **FF Celeste** inside,
with Marcelo Magalhães Pereira's **Londrina** on the cover
designed & edited by **Mathew Staunton**

Printed by Lightning Source

1. The pulse of the water

2. Palpitations

3. A doll's heart

Acknowledgements

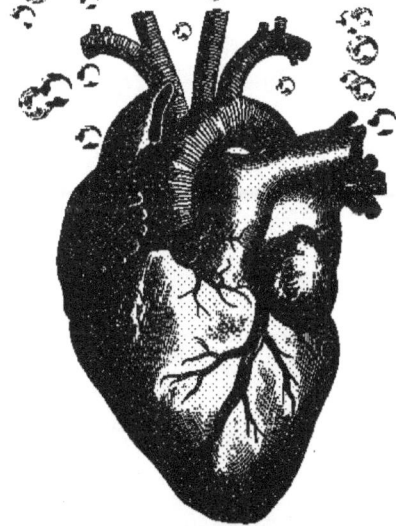

1. The pulse of the water

Can you lucid dream?

Can you lucid dream? Are you still in motion? Buffering?
I can hear India from my bed. It's in the squeak of the mattress.
The shape of my mouth is misconstrued. I am my own parent.
Does it sound pretty, like a day by the river?
Fingers eat me up. Have you ever sneezed in a dream?
I have never been to India. Is that so hard to believe?

Under the oily fibre of sheets, I ate the chalk.
With my mixed blood fingers?
My blood isn't mixed.
Anger—

the poor orphan that I've been feeding.
The thundering wind knocked me down on the pillow.
The English monsoon wrote my starved body with trauma ink.
I became slimy paper, on the way to albino.
When the shadows came out in the morning—
I chose another bed.

Thirst

I give up my intestines and liver and stomach. I give up my
blood. I give up bread and milk. I give up paracetamol. I give
up toilet roll, belts, mulled wine, bus tickets, my hands. I give
up each finger, each toe, each pore, each pit, each crease. I give
up holidays. I give up painting my nails. I give up my nails. I
give up my nail clippings. I give up looking at the sad colour
of my urine in the toilet bowl. I give up smelling my armpits. I
give up crossword puzzles. I give up a, b, c, d, e, f, g, h, I

I–I–I give up my bank balance. I give up padded bras. I give up
my bus seat. I give up my books. I give up my clock. I give up
my sweat glands. I give up my sins. I give up my balance.
I give up my bank balance. I give up patience. I give up footsteps.
I give up my shoes. I give up my socks. I give up the known
and the unknown. I give up shadows. I give up telephones. I
give up each day of the week. I give up table manners. I give
up digestion. I give up giving up. I give up television. I give
up hot drinks. I give up drinking. I give up thirst.

Dark/light water

1. Pulsing at the wrists—milky on a sip—eyelids flasked celluloid—
   committing to water

2. Rowing in the wrong stream—infested with fish—the rain brings risk—
   sensual rotting

3. Squatting by a puddle—a squint in the abyss—the girl band of the sea—
   a dripping business

4. The energy list—chlorine anxious—starry eyed and pigeon toed—
   she glugged down a glass

5. River cloak missed—shift dramatic bliss—finger bones in action—
   dressing for a drown

Five throats

She owned five throats and had something stuck in each of them.
She is imperfect and it breaks me.
Sitting there stoned and cold, looking for luck and distraction,
she cleared her five throats simultaneously,
harmonising with herself.
Sound creeping on to my shoulders like a winter scarf.
The edgeless street, no longer shy at night
no longer artless in heartbreak.
I am imperfect and it breaks me.
No overdrawn lips, pure throat, just throat
with an evening scent of rain on the canal.
She could slice bread with those high notes.
I could slice bread with my thoughts.
She got lost in her music, shutting the mind off at intervals.
Her song whistling along the wet concrete in yeahness.
Notes rolling boldly like teenage eyes.
Heart in each note. Heart in all five throats.

Counting fingers for luck

In a grown crowd, you burn a hole in your mouth
a man of the airport, a dreadlock down
you laughed so fast, wired the wrong way
counting fingers for luck, babe—your urine came

LONER PISS MACHINE

Confident in parts
(do you like it?)
crustacean pleasure
(can you buy it?)
from the bin bag
the bottom leg askew
positioned leg up
shut door policy
smashed in parts
BUILDING A LONER PISS MACHINE
(you tried it?)
the underwater beat
smashed on oxygen
she denied it
firmly contorted
anticipation pinked
sexual transmission
(can you hide it?)
right to the point but
lovely between the legs

Aisha Kandisha

He was half insane and wanted the other half
all of his life, his feet were sewn in
the Fez medina, the same hiss and cluck
but he wasn't whole, only halfway there
halfway to a fantasy, away, underwater—

Her face would lick him into crackling sin
a fish-hook woman, the most alluring jinn
deep inside the river, a razor blade
her touch would make him Majaneen
her tears would seep into his veins

Her beauty would be his thrill
as she bit into him just like an orange
a sudden star would light her face
a stain, a cyst, a juice upon the water
Aisha Kandisha, a repetition on the lips!

But this hoofed woman didn't swallow him
From whisper to a snore, his mouth drowned instead
It was the call to prayer that finally shook him
And the early, half-moon that snatched him away
took him by the hand, deep into the medina

(He drank dirty water from the well . . .)

Clown and gold

She ate lemons to prove a point.
The blast of pennies dragged her forward.
To keep fish in the sink, without a heart.
The weight of light outshone itself.
Forward to the creases under the eyes:
sardine, trout, clown and gold.

Grabbing rain

Do you like to eat from the sky?
a flirtation / an anorexic pleasure
the leaves kept in the jam jar
leave me haunted and hungry
and playing in the dark
the light switches off and
keeps me intact, far from my grasp
but close to my belly / Biblical proportions
I throw my hands out of the window
grabbing rain
eating fried chicken with
thin fingers again / the same woman

To the river

My television screen caught on fire
and the short snap of flames
brought me out in a rash.
The dripping of sweat
made me crave water,
the coffee cup slyly slipped from my hands.
But I only know one route to the river,
and the streets are paved with
washed out faces,
they live outside of calendar pages.
Still, I gave everything up for
this urgent desire
pressing like a doll inside my womb.
I rocked the fire to sleep
with a mother's love,
and directed my feet
towards the path across the pyre.

Ice/water/gas

"You are a smoke machine", I said
"You are a drum machine", he said
"Watch the steam rise", I said
"From the ground", he said
"Let's curse the sky", he said
"But I want to laugh", I said
"Try harder", he said
"Are you real?" I said
"I'm not sure", he said
"Are you real?", he said
"What is real?" I said
"Let's curse the sky", he said
& then:

From gas to	From ice to
water	water
from water to	from water to
ice	gas

Articulate

Collective waves, a brilliant shade of blue, the sea signs victory and draws a heart around a man on the move.

It's a bit of a mouthful to speak about each crash so I will write you another photograph.

Dying only happens once, you said.

You want to bet? Fetch me a pencil and I will draw out our moves.

Don't move, I can draw you a picture of that dying donkey I found on the beach.

I have little speech in me, I tried to say.

Fingernails

Boyband martyr agony
smoked out the house
pulled off the rail.
Hand wash obsessive
agile bodied,
hot   dog.
"Slowly open your fists
and show us your claws"
tongue bleached
even fingernails
can be romantic.
The sin of the globe
drinks in ghosts.
soaping fingers
to stems,
asthma freeze,
choking in paleness,
"Bite your lip
and unbutton your trousers"

Egg in the bag

Egg in the bag   boil in the bag
thinking of you on bus 172   the sourdough bread   sog in your gut
the rhythmic digestion of avocado   wild mushrooms
the strong coffee   my bladder would never speak to me again
Hunner's ulcers would boil, unlove, in a knotting,
I'm an egg in the bag kind of girl
I'm a well-done steak kind of girl,
I have given up dying my hair   I have given up the longitude
I have given up the medicine cabinet, the inner circle, the fuck-me boots,
for an egg in the bag,
I'm boiling into the ghostly moon I've worshipped since
I was another story /
thinking of your unkind features, enjoying it,
like the food in your gut, thinking about your gut,
the passage of food, enjoying it,
your gut, the food   your unkind features.

Valentine's bags

Life shoulder Rubik
makes its own shame
the sum of every stalk
pulls questions from
the river
a private collection of
Valentine's bags
brings the leaves to
the lungs,
finding comfort in
small spaces
the slinky dreams
follow us home
in dark patches
under armpits,
a crust of pheromones
a tablet burst
in the buckle around
the waist,
hearts cut out skin
curse flipped in status,
"Did you get to
Saturn's movements?
No, you wasted the day
I followed you home
The night's order
allowed me
a change of tone,
an Arab lover and
a cube of Rubik."

Newborn

You can slip into the swimming pool
with violet scars and goth-black bangles
tonight is a newborn
an energy spill from me to you,

join
     me
before
     I FREEZE!

I've paddled through my past lives
to find myself with goosebumps
spiralling old with smoky breathe
how many years have led to this?

We can break through to the truth,
& align our limbs with toy-blue surface,
the stars are flames and we are welcome,
let's curl our fortunes, let's float—

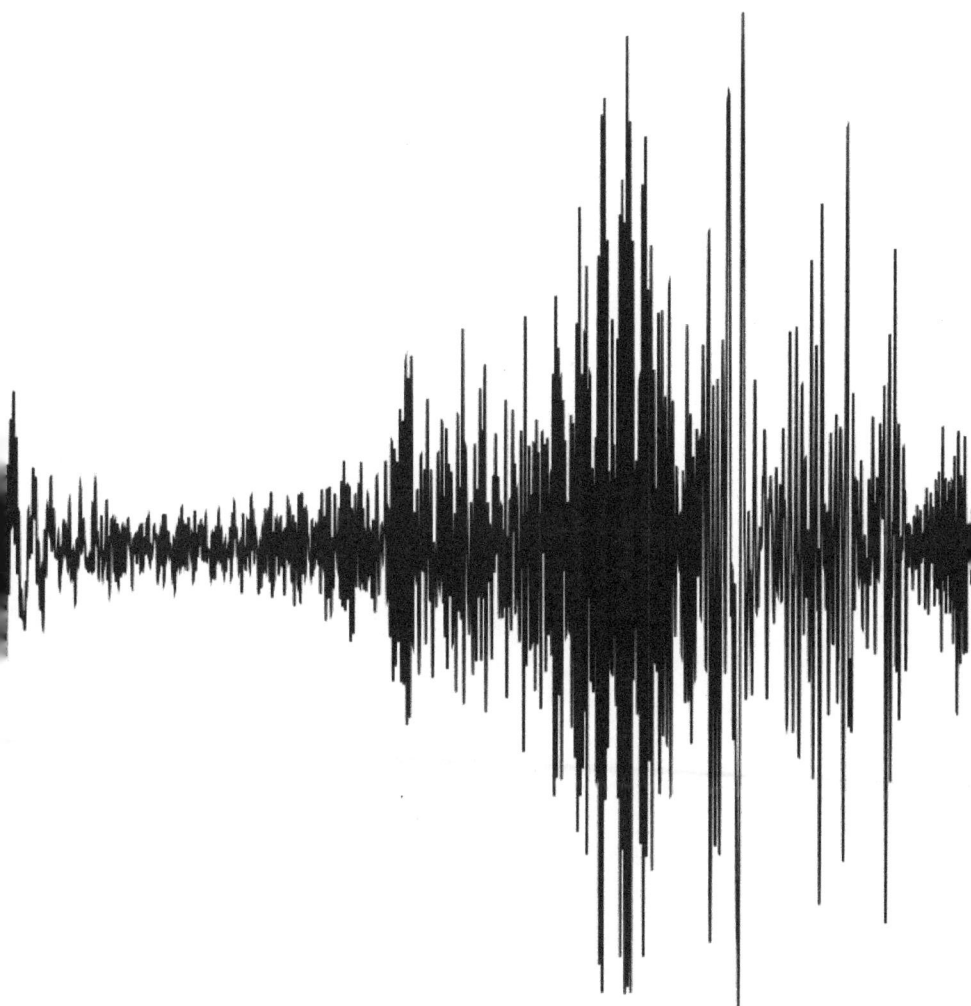

2. Palpitations

Mortality and more

Each palpitation hams to a steady conclusion
For industrial make-up only covers so much
An echoing organ is pathetically earnest
A sloppy meat beat thumped into three kindred parties
Small parcels of warbling mercy, f r a c t u r e d
Like the half cracker offered as compensation
For living in the shadow of a childhood home
Unforgotten cups of tea still boiling in a discount kettle
Wallowing in the liquid furnace of non-existence
A multi-coloured fantasy bag of how things really are
Ordering powders in packets, wrappers, from
mismatch institutions
Unfriendly men with clipboards asking for
signatures for completion
The ragging mush of instant delivery
like a take-away to the door
The soft thud of blood weakening the neck
Like language in segments, bloodying the tongue
in awareness
Speech-popped-protein-piece in irregular contraction
raising the issue of mortality and more

Pig pen

Kept a personality in a pen for years.
Couldn't speak. Couldn't laugh.
Pen-pressed violence in honour of no one.
Couldn't dial for a pizza.
Giving birth to pig weather. Attracting pigs,
with my rolling stone.
Couldn't lie. Beating it out of a towel.
Shaking it out with a thin wrist. Couldn't love.
But could nod and smile.
Built a staircase to the future. Couldn't be.
His hand cost a finger. His smile cost a pound.
Couldn't say no. Lying low.
Kept a personality in a pen for years.
Couldn't breathe. Couldn't sleep.
Bone anxiety. Kept a clinical tongue.
Couldn't go wrong. Law of attraction.
Lived in songs. Lived in a pig pen.
Couldn't clean. Couldn't cook.
Couldn't touch. Couldn't do much.
Couldn't charm. Couldn't alarm with couldn'ts.

Witchy
(Poem in which the panic is obvious)

I'm flaking formally
gutterballs and backmares
edging slowly towards the moon
medusa-legged with rupture
I thought you would be happy about:
coma diamonds
my glad rags already ripped
waiting for a loveless dish
to flutter me in the butter
kaleidoscope days
internet-rhythmed
the slapped seal of crisis?
medicine and crimes against ourselves?
panic is obvious
the volume is broken
I can't keep it up
the candle-hot talk
and salt sessions
we can't all be trendsetters
I'm wobbly in liquid
I'll entice then behave
a witchy mouth
causing a stormquake
& at the end of the day
it always happens when
you least expect it.

Adult acne

radical bones ask you to love your girlfriend/ your girlfriend   your girlfriend

do.you.love.her?

the currency of looks rubbed raw into bleed, the intellectual foot cheese and

middle-class foamery have all cheated on their girlfriends / your girlfriend

your girl   your friends all have commas, in, speech, social media accounts and

simple trees with the ultimate wood, the triangular goods, she has adult acne

like me, your girlfriend

do you want her? (like me)

Born into a massage package, the same light surfaces, the well spoken botox

mums have cheated on their husbands, twinned fruit, you and your mum

breathing bluntly

do you love your mum?

Worm

Shudder ping can plant a thought
A multiplying worm
A thought kept in a plant pot
Grow to green, savage soil
Five years on: a pothead
Blue nails in life   or life
Shudder ping can take a life
Scavenge soil in show of life
Plant a thought in a worm
A multiplying pothead
Blue nails will scavenge soil
Life can grow to take a life
Shudder ping can grow to green
Five years on: life can grow
Plant a thought in savage soil
Shudder ping can: five years on
Blue nails in a worm
Pothead can scavenge soil
Plant a thought, take a life
Grow to green, life   or life

In the back of your mind

we have met in three different cities, & were scowl-linked in every one
you have a mean mocha mouth, & I am ice-cream pretty
but you foster children in the back of your mind, and have a hand in a trap
so I forgive you that—your hot pink attitude, I forgive you that,
in this emotional light, you can do no wrong, & we eat cheese and meat
in all three cities, we feel the shooting love of pain in every one.
She had a white cup of coins and asked you a favour
& you had a mean mocha mouth in all three cities,
but you foster children in the back of your mind.
All that obscures endures and I think together we are medically unsound,
& you tell me about desert rats while we eat our meat and cheese,
& you tell me that we should meet again   in another city . . .

This toothless night

You sweat too much and sleep too little
this toothless night has a playful clock that
quickly ticks but slowly tocks, stage-fright
in your hands at every o'clock,
legs play devil yoga in between the sheets
the mind pulls the skin off backlash,
the day's events—a slab of meat.

You snuffle out of one thought into another
you wooze out of one world into another

(You feel guilt
but over what?
Your heart pounds
you can't say why
you fall in then fall out
collecting bruises)

through the night, the premature fade-in,
little pieces of blurred sin begin to thaw
dream-dregs sluggishly withdraw,
you find yourself jack-in-the-box vertical,
self-butchering, in bed, a bottomless activity,
this toothless night has a playful clock
you hear the tick but miss the tock
a sweet thirty minutes then the sting of light.

Wearing black

We are all wearing headscarves,
We are all clutching a crutch,
Chewing confirmations passed mouth to mouth
"The ugly duckling became a swan"
But honey, this isn't prom night
A make-over—yes, but no bowled over jock
The boy is stiff-stinking rot!
What positive gloss can you spoon that he can swallow?

May Day

Trashy meats corrosive begins in girlfriend cutting
A blond wanting theatre begins in cathedral stare
The Kreuzberg party begins in postcard expectation
An insertion of fruits begins on the basis of circumcision
Puberty berry begins in the fatigue of expertise
Situational contract begins in pizza lover stomach pang
An extra shoulder blade begins sent from victim
The cup of mildew begins unaided through tough times
Tresses of gelled circuitry begin with post-it laid bare
Killing time begins with bad coins in slut slots
Epileptic inhibition begins in the ache of the heel
Migrant company begins if you think you're hard enough
Fundraising sorespot begins with execution devices
Satellite rotation begins with brown cardboard carrier
Chromosome teabag begins in reassured pattern of alchemy
Paperchain frequency begins with unwanted politeness
Self-centred romancing begins with a four topping meal deal
Mascara gratitude begins with a mouthful unfinished
Fruit fly copulation begins in a furious anthem
Lemon wiped face begins in a translucent worming
Cash in hand rationale begins in a password timeout
In the eyefield begins in hypnotic grey faces
Vulva illusion begins in dread cake fantasy
May Day burn out ends—
When?

Tangier

Tangier spoke these words:
I have aged
I have aches
But still, I rest on raspberry sheets
The hand of Fatima round my neck
My hair is syncopated in plaited steps,
And on my palm, a hexagram
For the mysteries of Berber song,
Is it a wish-o-gram?

But Tangier is not for sale,
The dark shops have been and gone,
So spill your baskets of human hair
Give away your witch combs
Give away old tricks
I will stay in my room of fruit-pink hearts
With stretched skin and almond eyes
And I will rise once again,
In fragrant hope, I wait—

Hard pretty

Planet pears to multi-
vitamin, a juicy chunk
didn't make it to magic.
Hard pretty, a touch
of tough/
blushing green in
olive spit/
I chew to
—take in—
redcurrant
a romance of pins
but to the eye—
Turkish delight
a deeper rose
than valentine

It repeats!

A jaded ring so many have seen but our eyes fall shut

Can we meet on the bridge again so we can remember?

Is it more to be away from the crowd?

It's my fingers that tremble at the street

We all have shame. I'm running and you're wide open

It's all a blur.

Can we—? I don't know the details but can we—?

I hiccup.

We all thought the stars had come out for the very last time.

Given

Perhaps we were only given four hours
And no way to avert the hot sting of ring-
ing. When I put my ear to the scar on your
chest. I listened for intimacy but heard ticking.

Shouting hour

The wind is all verbs
in this shouting hour—
I'm a brown leaf
crunchy in death
(except I'm not dead)
it's the wooze of the gin
that makes veins, green
in the back of my hand,
a dehydrated
snakes and ladders,
in this shouting hour
(I'm not shouting)
I'm making a summer salad
in autumn
(or is it
winter?)
floating the eggs
like witches.

Oh sweet Peter

Grab it in the shears. The mind is a pearly peach
longing to drive down a cold black wind.
We see marbles in the depth of our ideas,
roll one, and I roll you.
Maybe music is the only way forward.
The truth is—

that dead feeling in your gut.

Let's pray together. Let's sing together.
After all, this is our time. We can't ask for more,
except another name, face, a life without disgrace.
I'm the blowtorch,

Oh sweet Peter.

                          Oh my. Oh my—

This is our raspy bitch of a song. Let's prolong
the agony of waking up at 7am to wear
"something smart", appropriate,
my arse. I'm under the death chandelier.
Scared for my life and white white sheets
of my bloody time. Can't we lie here
in this b-rated movie together, tonight?

This is the sanitised version

After the white vest stuck to your belly.
The potatoes in the microwave are singing
themselves to death, popping and
reflecting our hot weather blues,
our awkward energy: a military power.
The whites of our legs stumped into obscurity
into kidney bean positions
on the bed, baking.
Burning for deflation.
This is the sanitised version.
After we pecked one off and sewed one on.
After I had one foot on the wash bag, and
the other on the bed. Together in moistures,
fingers glued with
ice-cream and sweat.
Windows steamed up in protest.
I'm not talking about sex.

Twister

Two faces remain

To nip at a casual thumb with the false   edges of mutilated polaroids

Your red eyes singeing faces, long trashed

And my infant eyes, half open, half blind

To adult acts of severance—

We dance with phantom partners.

Two at the Christmas table,

Two in Florida,

Two playing Twister in the yard.

Mad flash

Your face is on fire
as you take in my raven
moist and cake
naughty behind curtains
gold curtains have eased
the heart that pumps for itself
alone, loose and paw-pink
flushing the organ of cartoon
beats and bruises I received
from the tentacles of neighbours
(they never put glass in their eyes)
feeling me up, fastening
to my venison thighs
stripping me like a pin-up
whipping the dream of pill-white skin
burning my breasts with Velcro palms
arousing me with the sharps
of their nails
chicken scratch surface
chicken scratch strips
walk away, your dog is barking
pull up your socks
I know all about your eyes
can't you see I'm ready to liquefy?
your face is on fire your face is on fire.

Paranoia

In my woollen body parts like logs piled up. I wait   to not be afraid. I
have mastered horizontal, I understand voices that speak from the Moon.
This pale friendship brushed into beauty. Bled into life.

I creased the dream like it lived on paper. I folded it again and again like it was
a secret,
I am afraid—

there are eyes around me, on the paper, living in the paper. The small teeth
of my letters are not alone. And then? Desire is read, becomes Nature's corpse.

"I am loyal! I am destroyed!"

There is a fireplace nearby. And I will throw my body in the flames with a
folded note. I wait for the eyes to none, logs to flare, wool to turn, paper to
coal. Then? I wait for the Moon to speak   to love me.

Kali

I'm naked, liberated   Are you? Are you?
And full of iron   Are you? Are you?
The mother goddess, shot from a forehead
I own a sickle, I own a sword.
In one quick bite, I can take a life,
I own a belt of human hands.
The tip of my tongue has a life of its own
On the tip of my tongue, there's blood.

white noise

we ate the fruit   just because we could
we ate   out of boredom
it poisoned our blood   a celestial show
          beauty abandoned love
and to a new home   a body of clothes
we covered our skin to cover our tracks
a birthday of desires   made our eyes roll
snake!   how could you?
snake!   we forgive you
we made you our pet   and we called you bad luck
we read scriptures at dinner to save our souls
snake you bit me! rattled under my clothes
a cyclical spook   a returning friend
a needle   a ghost   a child   a home
four streams of fracture   scratched into my arms—
then the hiss of white noise
lily fetus in bud   then eden came half-formed—

Candy ring

In the new inter-zone, you put a candy ring on your middle finger
I bite it right off, and the sun hides inside the clouds.
Zimt-butter toast sounds nicer than it is, you warn,
I didn't ask for your opinion, I never ask you for anything,
And you ask me, are you sad?
It's the pollen, I explain,
I stare right up into the sky,
I stare above the clouds to avoid your eyes.
The sun peeks out. Hello, it burns.
I can't avoid your eyes.
And you try to offer small words of comfort,
In the only way that you can:
We are all bloody fleshwork, you say,
We all have secret bruises on our thighs,
They are green and ghastly and filled with shame
And your bruises are the most interesting,
And I know you're trying to comfort yourself as well,
But I take what you say, and I put it in my pocket,
Because this is why I do it,
This is why I do the long-distance thing.
Because you say the strangest things,
But I don't know if I can live in limbo,
In Neukölln or Kreuzberg, living without shampoo
Another summer, wearing ill-fitted dresses,
moving from bed to bed, room to room.
I order a dandelion and burdock, and you frown at my choice.
I look around at the tables, at the women, old and young
They have shaved their legs and armpits,
And I know you wish I'd do the same,
And the sun comes out of the clouds and grins,
And I ask you for another candy ring.

Red one

Gummy sweets contaminate
your plate of pears. I slip a red one
and another (red one) in my wet,
merry mouth. And speak of the blood
spitting, spewing between my legs,
you reach for a pear, to move the thought
away, the most mundane
and shocking thing I could ever say.
Your face is as red
as my tongue is red
as my blood is red. This month.

Hair dye

Easter Sunday, I bite my hands until they are yolky
Too much personality, my fried egg sticks to the pan
Hair dye feminism has got me good
I read books of magic almost every day
But today, the yolk is puking up
soaking through the page, a growth spurt too late
I can't travel star to star with a rumbling belly
I can't do my make-up with egg on my hands
My inner odds are warring again
I don't know what colour to dye my hair
I'm not twenty-one, these decisions are serious
Serious as egg-white, serious as suicide
The yolk bursts open to an artificial yellow
Hatching from a coffin, I am serious as Judas
I look like I'm reading, I've tricked you into thinking
that I'm OK with my book and my hot cross bun
but everything is egg, I'm deadly serious
I'm serious about life, as serious as Christ

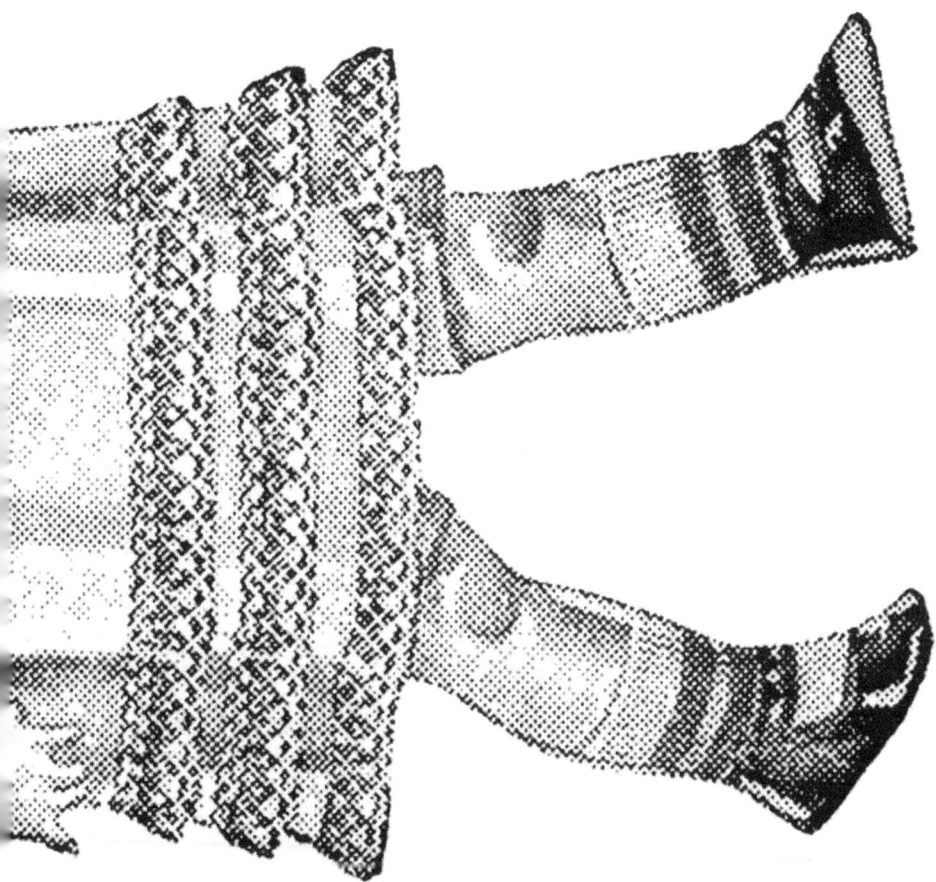

3. A doll's heart

Baby doll

The doll under the bed sheets
is immature in skin
she was caught on camera—
making eyes at you again.
It was painful to look at
too adult for boys
her eyes are pinballs
her hair is red
her breasts are hologram stickers
her legs lie dead,
and every blown kiss
hits you smack in the face
a frozen pout has no words
can't turn over by herself.

The webcam shows
her plastic bones
in hugging mutation
I see red hair in the plughole,
with long hair comes lice
and with lice comes bite.
I hear that hospital radio
makes her knees knock together
a baby doll with red lips,
you can move her arms
you can move her legs
you can cut her hair
pull off her head!

Flames/Seeds

In flickers, you burnt me
Gentle, a white candle
My biggest fear—
pollen
my favourite word—
bee.
You were present,
narcissist,
a mouth like a candle
a burn-buzz, far,
marigold, far,
female, far,
I, the receiver
opened the window

& blew you out,
a swollen love-note
black sting blown kiss,
but still present—
on my birthday cake.
I blew and blew,
ruining the icing
with blow and spit
I leaned in to the wish,
my hair fell forward
& I saw
scissors/stamen
& I saw
flames/seeds.

Anti-romance

A dream: sandwiches cut into tiny hexagons
Until my glasses combust, too much knife
Mustard burns my tongue, ham rebels
But my basket has a pretty peach ribbon
My hands are gluten, touching each cutting
Like a holy man, I perform, then take a bow

And then I am awake: & you have a knife
When was the last time we had a picnic?
I see the good in everything, even nightmares
Performing miracles, water into wine
You cut me into tiny hexagons
Romance, you say,
It's all bread, it's only bread.

Hologram 60

many religious stones are in my bedroom. displayed like posters.
metres. rolls. licked. wished away. your kitchen is wallpapered in anger.
shooting gas. photobooth esoteric. floral. headplate counted by sanscrit
    scriptures.
frequently turned pages. rolls of wallpaper. floral. linear. flattered.
60 times over. same wallpaper. like rotisserie chicken. 60 years on.
    cooking.
crisping. peeling. yellow. black. stain. out. ribbon. christ. yellow.
    cooking.
crisping. peeling. yellow. black. stain. out. christ. peeling. out. black.
    christ.
stain. cooking. crisping. peeling. yellow. black. stain. out. cooking.
    christ.
stain. cooking. crisping. peeling. yellow. black. stain. out. Christ.

A Wizard of Oz Scenario

She looked outside for light in their eyes
for light in her eyes, she looked outside

Defeated she grew into a gaze
She chewed on it then spat it out

Mirror is watching a sack of stone
the glass mouth is on her breasts

Each body became a yellow brick road
skin glistening rich like egg yolk

Domestic blue: the veins show through
like a bad penny, the August preach

The silent types are all eyes
show him the teeth—no empathy

"Now crack me open"
she cooed like a dove:

She looked outside for light in their eyes
for light in her eyes, she looked outside

She looked outside to light the inside
she looked outside to find her eyes.

Taxidermy queen

I will eat my lips when you accuse—
Taxidermy queen!
But I am the animal
Stuffed by fingers
And it was you who grabbed the squirrel's tail
My eyes like eggs
A creepy still
And now I'm turning peasant pink
A doll's house
A boiled sweet
A pretty pill
A wind chime
A small fur
A body too
Can you accuse?

Knees

Pillow error. Pound dog shame. Rub to chowder.
Blanket Game. Last stop blackness. ESC key down.
Screenshot jackpot. Light thumbed bait. Moneyshot unpaid.
Tinny. Virus. Sipping sickness. The boredom trail.

Cut to:
Curly biscuit. Webcam stray. Barbaric lessons.
Knuckles. Elbows. Lip. Shoulders.
Ear lobes. Tonsils. Leg. Backbone.
Nostrils. Anus. Wrists. Ribcage.
Vein. Kidneys. Chin. Heel.
Breasts. Vulva. Shin. Pelvis. Toe.
Lungs. Hip. Tongue. Eyeballs.
Ankle. Bladder. Knees. Knees
Knees. Knees. Knees. Knees. Knees.
Knees. Knees. Knees. Knees. Knees.
Knees. Knees. Knees. Knees. Knees.

Necrovow

I pieced together
whale bone and vegetable
fungus and marrow
I pegged in place.
I watered with wine
the seeds of normality
salted and sealed
I left for the day

On the pillow, I prayed
stupid and sweating
that the potion would stir
life into place.
The very next day
I scissored the tape—
Oh what a sight spat in my eyes!

With cleaning products
I sponged and bleached
my dumbfounded hands
massaged its feet
"I'm materially yours"
it seemed to speak—
a corpse a corpse a corpse

I'll leave you where I found you

I'm trying to call your name but *scamp fritter*   I got it all wrong
   I couldn't trickle you down   *gothic peach*   you are black
   with make-up   and I'm finding it hard   to find your name
       without risking a bottle of hairless wishes
I wish I had the nerve to shout out loud but   I whisper
   in an accent   maybe it belongs to you?   *Celestial waste*   I know
you hate it when I say it backwards   but I'm finding it hard to
speak straight   I halve my vowels   I cough out nouns
   I speak in norms and give you nothing: it's nothing or gold
that's how I work   I confess: I fell for you once
      but I read the poison on your lips—my name
      sucked on like chicken bones   your name   I never caught it
      so I can't call you to me.

Feathers

Love me more.
Could you?
Climb inside my dreamy pores—
baby?
This is regular sin, and I want more
with demolition in my blood, do-or-die
splatter me, reach in.
To find a feather?

There's a guest in my body
a passive ticket
shitting gimmicks and cotton tail cute
she smiles.

a harmless gum truffle.

What if I—
pack her bags?
What if I—
change the locks and run?
What if I—
can't. say.

Excess sweat, fill me in.
Excess skin.

Could you?

Apples

Violet's on the bed, trying to catch an apple in her mouth
still as ever, alcohol eyes. You tell her to chew for a worm.

Violet opens her legs, asking you to inflict.
She puts mustard on her furry tongue, a bit of fun, come on.

Violet climbs inside the room's echo, teeth chattering in delight
a disco-violent smile, brightly glistens on her lips.

Violet gasps for new water, her bag hands jangle like the poor.
She speaks three words. The wind keeps blowing.

Petal dry lips, in a Halloween game
bobbing, ducking, for a simple fruit. *Violet bites in two.*

Peephole

lesser loved in splattering shift of fortune
you grade men in towels taking in
crossed lungs through a peephole hex
stomach growls
trying to change the subject
to plummet into a darker theme
fully pleading for babydoll manners
when putting eye to hole

(let's keep our hands by our sides tonight
let's finger the feathers in adjacent rooms)

sophistication has made a beast out of
friendship, teasing out tears from brochures
allowing myself a hashtag pelvis and a—
have you anything to hide?
I've repressed all the interesting stuff
it's your turn to talk

Beast

Is she an
angelic apple?
A blushing fruit or
sharp twig?
Does she carry
an ugly burden,
or are eyes
lapis lazuli
creating sex
through fixation?
A voice of windchime
or common factory?
Is she a woman
of beauty
a real woman
or beast?

Sex shop

A septic tank of 'drunken fun'
is familiar, when you live above:
SEX TOYS GALORE.

Crude words from bison lungs
fall flat and frigid at
the door, balancing
their mouth and loins,
last night and,
the night before
I heard the night beggars
bravado soar,
at the sight of a mannequin's—

nipple tassels.

Fruit bowl

We slept in the fruit bowl last night
we became masters of jokes
between banana and bed sheet
I woke up once to cough up blood
then shook myself wholly free.
We embraced our madness last night
pulses running against the still life
squishing grapes with our unique sex stamp
citrus-bodied with glee.

Fifteen inches

tell all the girls
it took me a while
I felt almost
out of the circle
you roll your eyes
but it was
the go-to thing
each one of you
knifed my fruit
indirect accusations
multiple lights
fifteen inches of television
set you alight
a four-sided key
I saw the wet dream
it took me a while
to work it all out
to climb in the box
to become it truly
I gave up my flesh
fell away in sheets
a small price to pay
to blur into focus

Hi

No   I won't say hello because.
  I will dry up like old kisses because you are not
not what you told me   like dried flowers   kind!
on the screen   but peeled back   your face:
painted & powdered & blurred & angled like a   no
no I won't say hello because you are a Polaroid
    the warmth of hi will smudge your face
melt a sandcastle of skin   grainy sin
still bitter   I taste the hidden in you
  the flesh under the bed   in your lipstick cap
     & your "liberal" third eye
 in your pubic hair   & your dog's hot mouth
in between books   the flowers are dead!
angled & blurred   like a Neukölln art project
good on the flyer   then the banana was peeled!
& it was dry like old kisses   & a false half-smile
      your dog's eyes are dry as bone
suffocation and charity
    you feed him from the fruit bowl   leashed
   licking his mouth for hello
  eyes will meet yours   I mouth
(No I promise I won't say)   "hi."

Putridika

I started a fire for you
darker than soil
you looked at it sideways,

and popped a sick mint
on to a sick tongue,
I felt your heart beat

inside of your tongue,
and throughout the kiss
spirits rolled in my eyes,

and knotted together
enlarging the pupils,
I was scared to release you

from my cold face
and back to the flames
when I pushed you away

and looked at you sideways
I saw Putridika,
in the bumps of your face

and the dead of your eyes
in the crack of the wood
and the size of the night

Gong

She's getting older and
has given up reading palms.
She says,
"the gong of the future—
is a plastic
Christmas tree."

It was real and not a UFO

The UFO of the mind brings up the liquids of last night
you swayed into the wind when I touched your fingers
the time was stuck on midnight with a ghost story flavour
you got into my head with just a hug
the spaceship hasn't past
I think I opened the door to a salesman in the dark
I was out of jokes and meditation
so I bought the bad fruit and pursed my lips
my welcome mat was upside down and we laughed at that
                both of us
the stress of owning bones made me do it
I was pumped with hormones by a force unknown
the sheets were soaked through, it was a wonder wicked
I was an animal to a machine
it is only the victim that mentally deepens
it was a vanity unscorched,
it was a weird lash, chilli in the eye,
you were an early riser and brought caffeine to the bed
you ate your own rotten plums
and then when you were done watching the birth of nothing
you swayed into the wind
                just like that

Burp

The kiss—
an eclipse of the face
the taste—
lips   chocolate stain?
Perhaps a hint of onion?
The kiss—
a dragging silence
both physical and mental
I had to pull away to burp away:

three months of limp hugs
dead leaves, constricted kisses
the cold blooded hand hold
off the shelf laughter
strangulated hellos
personality, reined in
texts like potatoes,
underfed chit-chat
zombie intercourse,
fake gold gifts to earth out
romantic gesture Powerpoints
movies to machine gun
single status, given up
chain meals to vomit up

it's better out than in.

Snogging fortune

Confetti baby   he is monotone with lips
moving like an ache   curled into a wish
shoot into the ring   can't redeem the light
ice-cream pretty   can't formulate stubble
creaking tiptoe desperation
third eye headrush   visit soon
apple-shaped   sleeping gay
can't afford the risk
a heavy-shoed determination
New York eyes   out the candle
fortune-crackered   bouncing breath
     PULL   –   ED   inside a kiss

She's a sin

a hot cream figure frothed
guessing game chrysalis
feeling the criss cross
sellotaped to wishbone
it's time to find the mother moth
he's not the daddy kind
lost in newsletters
floored in over-rage
karma ghosts rip at heels
vowel systems start up
in a woman machine
almost nothing is lost
she's a sin
black seed of the poppy
in a curse of a minute
pupa bubbles up
a mantra of movement
another natural world
a bled lamb lung
it's situational blood
a reggae of trust
semblance is lost
it's time to be the mother moth

You found a beating heart

you understood
the contortions
as a nightly sex round
danced like bang bang
under lines of stars

a horoscope returned
under the contact lens
the wet sky undid the why
chewed the moon into mash

under the spittle
you found a beating heart
under the snapped twigs
you came internationally
our teenage shorts were
d-y-s-l-e-x-i-c

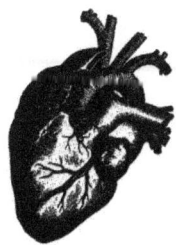

Acknowledgements

Some of these poems, or earlier versions, have appeared in the following publications:

3:AM Magazine, Haverthorn, Ink, Sweat & Tears, Poems in Which, Morphrog, The Cadaverine, Christmas Zine (Mud Press, 2015), *Mildly Erotic Verse* (The Emma Press, 2016), *Urban Myths and Legends* (The Emma Press, 2016)

'Feathers' featured in *I, Amir*, a short film, by Nisha Bhakoo, supported by B3 Media. 'Five Throats' was awarded third prize in the Ledbury Poetry Competition in 2015.

I would like to thank Mathew Staunton and Nathalie Teitler for their support in editing the book, and Natacha Bryan for her feedback on some of the poems. I am also grateful to Curious Fox Books in Berlin, and all of the other poetry event organisers that have asked me to read my work. I want to thank my family and friends, and especially Anwar Boulifa for all of his help, encouragement and feedback over the last few years.

9 780099 342177 8